The Gift of Time
Poetry Collection

Susan P Doherty

© 2024 All rights reserved. Susan P Doherty

978-1-915502-71-1

All intellectual property rights including copyright, design right and publishing rights rest with the author. No part of this book may be reproduced or transmitted in any way including any written, electronic, recording, or photocopying without written permission of the author. Published in Ireland by Orla Kelly Publishing. Images from the author. Cover design by 2funkidesign.com.

Orla Kelly Publishing,
27 Kilbrody,
Mount Oval,
Rochestown,
Cork,
Ireland.

Contents

Dedication v
About the Book vi

Introduction 1
Father's Day 3
Heaven Sent 4
The Day the Music Died 5
Broken 6
Shedding a Tear 8
The Little Robin 9
The Rose 10
The Book of Life 12
The Gift of Time 13
Losing You 14
A Tender Love 16
Tomorrow's Rainbow 18
The Mirror Image 20
A Dark Reflection 21
Anchored by the sea 22
The Dark Cloud 23
No Regrets 24
Under the Moonlit Sky 25
Life without You 26
My Heavenly Dream 27
Autumn 28
Halloween 30
Christmas Magic 31
The Christmas Angel 32
Gathering around the Christmas tree 33
The Last Goodbye 34

My Irish Maiden 36
Imperfections 38
The Fitness Machine 39
The Whisper 40
New Year Hopes 41
School days 42
Walk With Me 43
Footprints in the snow 44
Dancing with your Shadow 46
The Lullaby 47
A Time to Fly 48
The Waterfall 50
The Epitaph 52
Farewell to another Year 53

Acknowledgements 54
About the Author 55

Dedication

I would like to dedicate this book to the memory of my dear dad Eamon Doherty who sadly passed away on 2 March 2023.
Rest in Peace.

Blessed to have had you in our lives
Devastated you are no longer here with us
Missing you every day and trying to be strong
Rest easy with the angels in your heavenly place

About the Book

The Gift of Time Poetry Collection is a book of 40 poems that will take the reader on an emotional journey through the various stages of life including the beginning of new relationships, perhaps first experience of love and romance, to lifelong relationships, then touching on loss of a loved one and the deep felt grief that follows. Highlighting the fragility of life itself, recognising the need to make the most of every moment of time that we get to experience from seeing each new sunrise to cherishing time spent with family and friends. Learning to be happy within ourselves both physically and spiritually not focusing on perceived imperfections and being self-critical based on what we see on social media. The poems are not based on any real life situations however, each of the poems will take the reader on their own individual and personal journey resonating from their own life experiences. A number of the poems included link specifically to the beauty and often mystery of nature and how it is closely intertwined within the branches of life and supports us with emotional healing. Taking time out of our busy lives not chasing after material things instead realising where our priorities should be and focusing on fulfilling our dreams.

Introduction

The Gift of Time Poetry Collection invites the reader to experience a range of poems that focus on the gift of life itself and how precious this is and with the stark reminder that this life is ours for a limited time. Making the most of what we have, enjoying the beautiful seasons and the mystery and wonders of nature from the beautiful rainbows to the moonlit skies and magical waterfalls allowing us to take time out to experience the serenity of life. Enjoying family occasions and celebrations, gathering together indulging in happiness and immense joy and laughter such as at Christmastime. Accepting challenges in our life when the dark cloud casts overhead bringing huge personal devastation to our door, unimaginable grief due to the loss of a close family member or loved one. Wondering if we will ever be able to recover fully from the heartache and pain. A few of the poems invite us to look at our awareness of self-image and perceptions of what we and others should look like based on social media influence. We are asked to look at self-acceptance and readers are encouraged to spread their wings and grasp all opportunities that come their way putting away their fears of failing, casting away unwelcome shadows. A number of the poems show us that we have choices in many aspects of our life as we start each day with a new and relatively blank page.

Father's Day

Today we get to spend some quality time with our dad
Precious moments for which I am truly glad
A time to express our appreciation for all he has done
Ensuring our family life has been a wholesome one

A day of sadness for the dads that are no longer in our midst
Sadly the angels had them on their heavenly list
Missed so much and many will be shedding a tear
Fond memories in our hearts we hold dear

Heading out to work and bringing home his pay
Ensuring that we were looked after in every way
Caring and supporting us through each stage of life
Doing his best to steer us clear of misfortune or strife

Teaching us to ride our bikes whilst praying we didn't fall
Heart-warming smiles when we finally mastered it all
A keen gardener keeping the lawns so neat and trim
The tidy hedges and fences maintained to perfection by him

Showing his love of music and dance by legends of his time
Creating so many happy evenings that were sublime
Sharing his stories of growing up and happy times of old
Reflecting on vintage family history that needed to be retold

Developing our knowledge in preparation for life to make the right choices
Encouraging us to achieve our potential and trust our inner voices
Enjoy today dads hope it brings you much deserved joy and pleasure
Thank you for making so many memories that we will always treasure.

Heaven Sent

The appearance of a beautiful white feather is a welcome sight
Many believe it's heaven-sent from a departed family member
A sign of closeness of a loved one as they watch over us
Letting us know that they are safe with their heavenly family
Offering hope that one day we will be together again
Soothing the pain and anguish of the bereaved
Comforting and easing feelings of regret and perhaps guilt
Restoring warmth and calmness to the broken-hearted
A powerful gift of healing and providing release
A special delivery of love and energy shared from above

The Day the Music Died

The day you left us was when the music died
Our hearts were broken as we openly cried
People say the passage of time will ease the pain
We know that family life will never be the same again

An overwhelming silence and emptiness now exists
As the void from your missing presence continually persists
You loved to play music by your favourite artists
Listening intently and humming the lyrics

As your fingers pressed confidently on the accordion keys
Moving the bellows in and out with such precision and expertise
Gentle movements creating wonderful rich sounds
Your skill for learning new music held no bounds

Memories of younger days playing along with your friends
Your music entertaining and lifting spirits of all those present
Encouraging people to get up and dance
Slowing it down for couples to have a little romance

Classical, Irish Traditional, Folk, Jive, seasonal, a wide array
A kind and gentle person using your gift in a very special way
Talent and skills developed and expertly tuned from your youth
A wealth of memories of your music is our everlasting proof

We imagine you're now playing music with the angels each night
With your heavenly halo shining ever so bright
No doubt trying out new melodies entertaining your divine audience
Providing comfort and joy to others in abundance

Broken

The adrenaline was flowing and I accelerated, loving life and being me
Life was good, I was young and completely carefree
My world froze beyond my youthful comprehension that day
The dreadful crash that impacted on my life so horrifically

It happened very quickly, as I was just cruising along
Singing along to the sound of my favourite artists and songs
The beat blasting in my ears blocking the swish of the autumn breeze
My bike negotiating the road surface with precision and ease

My memory of the incident isn't very clear you see
The bike disappearing forcibly from beneath me
I recall being hurled into the air, no longer in control of my body
Then excruciating pain as I hit the tarred road heavily

Screaming in agony, terrified and thinking I was going to die
Moving in and out of consciousness as the cold dampness gripped me
Not realising that this was my own blood gushing out profusely
I could hear the sound of sirens and voices nearby but not clearly

Strong hands began to lift me and ask for my name and details
I was replying but I couldn't hear any sound as my voice fails
I hadn't seen the car coming, just having felt the impact as it enfolded
Having overtaken a lorry and ended up on my side of the road

A few weeks later they woke me from an induced coma state
Feeling very afraid, disorientated and somewhat irate
The doctors explained the extent of my injuries
The list was painfully drastic and really lengthy

My body and brain were damaged extensively
Impaired vision, unable to speak properly
No longer going to be able to walk or ride my motorbike
Having lost one leg completely and the other severed below the knee

My hands and arms had been fractured and severely crushed
Rehabilitation would give slight movement, a real plus
The startling reality that life was never going to be ok again for me
Wheelchair bound and dependent on others until eternity

I didn't know how I was going to cope
My body and mind as I knew them, were so broken
Doctors and my friends all said how lucky I was to survive
I'm not sure in my current state that I would agree

I question why I'm left alive like this daily
My mind and body are scarred mentally and physically
My friends tend to visit me now much less frequently
It isn't much fun to be hanging around me presently

My life seems to have been shattered instantly
My precious identity thrown away so recklessly
I long to experience the freedom of being on the road
Clearing my mind of all this mental debris

Shedding a Tear

As the tears begin to silently fall
It's not a sign of weakness at all
Often hidden as it shows vulnerability
Expressed in times of human difficulty
Closely linked to the emotions of the heart
Triggered by strong feelings of sadness or joy
An essential part of the bereavement process
Often a powerful release when suffering or in pain
Cleansing of the soul, shedding negative energy
Assisting in our physical and mental recovery
Running freely after periods of laughter
A sign of much happiness and hilarity

The Little Robin

A fascinating little bird that endears itself to everyone by its presence
A special little outdoor friend adding some mystery in essence
Curiously following you around the garden, mischievous in its quest
With its bright sparkling eyes and little red-coloured breast

Twisting and turning its little head this way and that
Trying to communicate with you and have a little chat
A busy little creature hopping back and forth fluttering its tiny wings
What secrets does it hold and special news or message does it bring

Sometimes getting brave and coming close to your side
Hoping to get a little treat, waiting with anticipation for you to provide
Especially when winter arrives and it shelters from the bitter cold
Relying on people's generosity as food becomes difficult to unfold

Often thought to be a sign that a loved one is nearby
Letting you know they are ok and encouraging you to be happy
Santa's little helper reminding children to be well-behaved and kind
So that on Christmas morning a special surprise they will find

The Rose

The Rose is one of nature's endearing creations
A symbol of love and comfort fitting for all occasions
Given as a gesture of kindness or a thank you present
Delicate flowers, velvety and soft, infinitely elegant

Comforting and rich in their presence at a sad event
Nurturing through grief and despair believed to be heaven-sent
Shared at the graveside an expression of final embrace
Carefully placed close to our loved ones everlasting place

Prominently positioned at weddings and joyous events
Taking centre stage in bridal bouquets with heartfelt intent
Beautifully scented, dignified and radiant bouquets
Stunningly presented in Church decorative displays

Petals dancing elegantly in the summer breeze
Proving a magnetic attraction for the butterflies and bees
Floral arrangements shaped large and small, guaranteed to excite
Many varieties with their precious array of colour, such a delight

The Book of Life

The journey through life is like a book
Filled to the brim with so many chapters
Representing each stage of your life
The cover often masking what is hidden underneath

There is an opportunity to begin a new page each day
Essentially starting off blank but filled easily
Making choices as to what it could possibly contain
Venturing into the unknown but with everything to gain

As children we are innocent and usually carefree
Developing our individual personalities as we grow
Seeing how far boundaries may be pushed
Yet dependent on guidance from seniors and peers

Our interaction with others through work and school
Putting plans in place to achieve positive future goals
Being a team member with everyone making their contribution
Ensuring important tasks and situations reach their conclusions

Time spent well with friends and family, enjoying life and having fun
Being role models and not making judgements that can't be undone
Ensuring your book of life although unique, will be affordable to everyone
Hopefully in the future it will be seen as an interesting and worthwhile one

The Gift of Time

Each new morning that we experience is a gift of time
Offering the opportunity to be creative and to shine
Often we have so many plans there just aren't enough hours
Constantly racing against the clock, under pressure to achieve

Not taking the time to see the precious things around us
Always in a hurry and unable to spare a moment of your time
It's important not to get stuck in memories of times gone by
Especially where there has been family strife or difficulty

Acknowledging the passage of time as we grow older
Sadly time moves forward so swiftly, catching us unaware
Instead cherish time spent with our friends and family
Take the time to recognise accomplishments and successes

Make the most of each day fulfilling your dreams
Sharing your gifts and supporting others
Recognising life's fragility and its limited availability
As eventually our final minute in time will arrive

Losing You

As we lie here in the hospital bed side by side
Trying to be strong and remain upbeat
Wrapped up in the beauty of your presence
Our hearts filled with contentment and warmth

When I first saw you it was the answer to my dreams
With your dark brown hair and blue-green eyes
Having met at a family wedding day
Seated at the same table, held captive in a way

Initially the conversation was reserved and quite dry
Gradually our confidence grew and we happily chatted
We kept in contact and love blossomed beautifully
We had a good happy life as husband and wife

We're together twenty years and have rarely ever fought
Not blessed with children, memories of losses never to be forgot
Sharing precious moments together and with friends and family
Cherished memories of adventures will remain with me forever

As you bore your pain so quietly never did you complain
Knowing deep in your heart that it would win in the end
As the cancer took hold it was determined to stay
You battled so hard to beat it trying every treatment and remedy

We watched helplessly as your once athletic frame wasted
It was difficult to see you lose your independence
The doctors and nurses were so kind offering care and honesty
Keeping us informed but also making us aware of the reality

Everything is very peaceful as I hear you breathe slowly
We watch the stars dazzle in the Midnight sky
I know it is getting closer, your time is slipping by
Reality hinting that soon I will have to let you go

Only your face reflecting the inward strain
You tell me the time is nearing for your journey's end
Having asked for forgiveness and made your peace with God
Asking him to grant your heavenly leave

A Tender Love

You caught my attention as you made your way through the crowd
Beautifully dressed with your long, flowing red-coloured hair
At first you didn't see me as you chatted freely to your friends
I couldn't take my eyes off you while trying not to stare

I was instantly drawn to you causing a strange stirring in my heart
I wondered if I had the courage to ask you to dance
Would I be able to handle any rejection of my clumsy advance?
Afraid to come across as foolish, trying not to rush things and keep calm

At that moment the music slowed to a more romantic pace
I realised it was now or never and plucked up the courage
As I came to close to you, you glanced my way and smiled
The lights were causing your blue eyes to dazzle in a magical way

I nervously asked you to accompany me on to the floor
You took my hand in yours as we slowly made our way
My heart was filled with warmth and beating quite rapidly
We danced well together and the conversation flowed easily

As I leaned forward and asked you if it would be ok for a kiss
Our bodies fitted so comfortably together, a moment of pure tenderness
The chemistry between us causing butterflies and nervousness
Unmistakable desire to spend more time with you romantically

We agreed to meet again and shared our contact details
Sending texts to each other almost every day for many months
Getting to know more about our interests, work and everyday lives
Growing closer and fonder of each other as time progressed

Then suddenly things changed and messages became few
No explanation as to why you no longer desired me, I had no clue
I had naively grown attached and fallen for your charm
The longing gradually eased and for the future I'm much better armed

Tomorrow's Rainbow

As the tears once more begin to fall uncontrolled
The feeling of deep sadness and emptiness unfolds
A sign of weakness not to be shared or publicly shown
Afraid of letting the shutters open and entering the unknown

The sheer burden of it all making life seem terrible
It sometimes becomes overwhelming and unbearable
Tiredness of constantly putting on a positive face
Afraid to trust or letting the real you surface

Living an unfilled life, void of any comfort or care
No closeness of a loved one or being part of a pair
Seemingly destined to be alone, a harsh reality
Not realising your potential and untapped ability

Accepting your part in life's undetermined destiny
Trying to look forward, searching for life's remedy
Cherish the wonders of each tomorrow's rainbow
As a special wish granted may open a new window

The Mirror Image

Standing in front of the mirror gazing at the reflection I see
Glancing at the image and thinking to myself furtively
I let my mind begin to critique everything negatively
Staring in surprise, surely that person really can't be me

I wonder is this because the mirroring isn't how I imagined it would be
I closely examine the image with a heavy heart and deep-set frown
Taking account of the wrinkles and body shape, giving it a dressing down
Feeling disheartened, deflated and somewhat ashamed

Putting pressure on oneself to look a certain way
Taken in by media portrayal of what looks trendy and is ok
Determined no matter what the cost to try and fit in
What body shape is acceptable and meets with public opinion

Not realising the reflection is just a map of my life's journey
Experiences gained through interactions with family and friends
The pathway we've shared hasn't always been plain sailing
Travelling along while negotiating many bends and rough terrain

Sometimes veering off track due to a change in life's plans
Choices made perhaps not always easily explained
Instead of nurturing my self-perceived imperfections and limitations
Accepting the person I have become and finding happiness within

A Dark Reflection

Sitting by the fireside listening to the logs crackling
Reflecting on time spent with family during times gone by
Many memories and visions of faces I used to know
As the warmth from the burning embers set my face aglow

A house that holds echoes of voices with happiness abound
Cherished moments of family singing, such a wonderful sound
Children relaying stories with heart-filled excitement close to overflow
Warming their cold little hands and toes after playing in the winter snow

Suddenly my body trembles, shivers running down my spine
Memories triggered of a never to be forgotten harrowing time
Coming out as each shift ends with blackened faces covered in dust
Eyes squinting in the early morning sun as they try to adjust

Working down the cold, dark tunnels day after day, night after night
Tackling the coalface guided with only small amounts of artificial light
The explosion that day, shouts and screams, such terrifying sounds
Lifted off my feet as all around me collapsed and I fell to the ground

I slipped into a state of semi-consciousness, confused and filled with fear
Making me frightened for the welfare of my colleagues, friends so dear
Everything around me seemed to have gone so quiet and dark
When I awoke a few days later in hospital, the reality was stark

As the horrific news was relayed to me that I was the sole person to survive
The death of so many hardworking men leaving their young families deprived
The scars of that devastating event remain with me, my permanent state
As I lost my eyesight and live in total darkness since that fateful date

Anchored by the sea

Surrounded by the deep blueness of the sea
As it stretches out way beyond what my eyes can see
The sun's rays reflecting on the surface causing it to shimmer
Dazzling magnificently under the beautiful light of summer

Occasionally moving along forcefully and loudly
The waves rise high and batter against the rocks ferociously
Surfers riding the waves enjoying the early morning swells
As they use their skills while enjoying the spills and thrills

Seated close to the beautiful pebbled and sandy beach
I watch as the tide washes inwards from the coastline
Sometimes moving calmly and quietly towards me
Peacefully observing its glory and mystery

Offering a buoyant platform for fishing trawlers and yachts
Protector of the marine creatures, many hidden deeply beneath
Often only observed when curious divers seek lost treasure
Whales and dolphins freely swimming, offering me such pleasure

I've always been drawn to the sea, knowing it was my destiny
Having been a sailor for all my youthful years, living so freely
Unable to move now as my wheelchair is anchored in the sand
This helpless feeling sadly compelling me to a life on dry land

The Dark Cloud

As the dark cloud begins to descend
Its deep shadow shows no end
Casting gloom and dismay
Leaving upset and destruction in its way

An unrelenting and disrupting force
Crossing boundaries and showing no remorse
Blowing a bone chilling breeze
Causing you to shiver and feel ill at ease

Making poor choices and leaving a mess
Causing much anguish and distress
In time the dark cloud will be overcome
Goodness will be accomplished and all suffering undone

No Regrets

Each morning being fortunate to experience the gift of the rising sun
A daily reminder of how precious life is and truly cherished by everyone
Having to weather the storms and holding firm to personal values
Bravely stepping out from the crowd seen as challenging and misconstrued

Dealing with other people's opinions, jealousy and enduring personal attacks
Having said things deemed unforgiveable, unwilling or unable to retract
Speaking ill of others tinged with hatred and negativity
Not offering the hand of forgiveness or voicing words of apology

Regrettable actions undertaken previously, longing to relive those moments again
A strong desire to turn the clock back, to deal with our embarrassment and shame
Putting up barrier walls to protect ourselves against rejection and uncertainty
Realising how short life can be, grasping the windows of opportunity

As the sun sets each night being able to relax and sleep easily
Not feeling anxious or unnecessarily weary
Living your life independently, filled with honesty and being free
With no regrets, what ifs, buts or maybes

Under the Moonlit Sky

Sit with me a while, I've been waiting for you so patiently
Talking and sharing our many youthful memories
As the stars glisten in the moonlit sky
I look upon you and admire your dazzling beauty

Realising how lucky I have been
As you gently slip your hand into mine
Being with you makes me so happy and free
No pretence, I'm able to be the real me

My heart is filled with such warmth and glee
The sparkle of your deep blue eyes, watching closely
Reflecting in the moonlight as I hold your face in my hands
I long for your companionship, only you can understand

I remember the first time I met you in our special place
Our silhouettes dancing under the night sky, nature's romantic space
Passionate moves, so much loving in our own way
Sharing our secrets and dreams, escaping from reality

Such intimacy and closeness, lifetime bonds being created
A shared vision of contentment, both of us feeling truly elated
A future planned spending the rest of my life with you seems so right
Wrapping you in my arms protecting you from the coldness of the night

Life without You

Will there ever be a time when the tears no longer flow
How will I ever get used to life without you, I just don't know
I miss you terribly, each day is unbearable since you breathed your last
Feeling totally despondent, bereft and downcast

As the waves of grief constantly rise to the surface
Threatening to overwhelm, pushing me towards the precipice
I'm trying to keep moving forward, being strong
How will I cope or find the strength to carry on

As the angels carried you away that fateful day
A huge piece of my heart was torn away
My heart is heavy and filled with such anguish and pain
So many things to say, longing to hear your voice again

Broken, shattered, never to be repaired
As I think fondly of all the good times we shared
Family life will never be the same again as I look at your empty chair
Longing for you to make an appearance, knowing you can no longer be there

Your bond with me was so precious, I didn't want you to leave
Knowing that one day we will meet once more, is my only reprieve
Living without you is so difficult, it's hard to explain
The silence and emptiness, a huge void in our lives that forever will remain

My Heavenly Dream

Holding you so close to me
Warm vibes radiate as two beautiful souls meet
As the soft music plays a familiar melody
I can feel the rhythm of your heart beat

Feelings between us incredibly strong
A lifetime together as forever we belong
Enchanted from the first moment by your beauty
Your zest for life and laughter, such natural purity

A lifetime spent together as we cherished each day
Creating a lifetime of memories in our special way
Building our home as a legacy for our precious family
Sadly I lost you as God chose you to pave the way

Time has passed and I'm now enfolded in your arms safely
Time to move forward as our heavenly places are ready
Blessed that we are united once more, sealing our destiny
Grateful that we will celebrate together for eternity

Autumn

Summer's leaves falling off the trees
Swept off their stems by the light autumn breeze
Their colours changing to golden yellow, red and brown
Rustling through the air and falling softly on the ground

The branches of the trees emptied of their foliage leaving many bare
Squirrels scurrying around gathering the acorns that have been blown everywhere
The sun comes up more slowly each morning and its rays don't glow as bright
Daylight dwindles and darkness falls earlier, bringing on the night

The flowers no longer displaying their bright beautiful colours and sweet fragrance
Bees getting ready to hibernate, butterflies and insects reducing their presence
Hedges and apple trees bursting with their abundance of fruit and berries
Providing sufficient food for the birds ensuring they do not perish

Nature appears to be slowing down, getting ready for the new season
Temperatures dropping down and the eerie sounds of the wild geese leaving
People spending less time outdoors as gardens become easier to maintain
Farmers bringing the animals inside to shelter from the strong winds and rain

Leaving more time for walking through the forest trails or visiting the sea coast
Experiencing the wonderful seasonal changes of our autumn host
Nature seems to becoming less busy making way for a time of calmness
Encouraging us to slow down, rebalance and welcome its tranquil stillness

Halloween

Halloween arrives each year on a cold and dark October night
A chance to have some spooky fun going on ghostly tours by torchlight
With all kinds of characters jumping out of the shadows for our amusement
Anticipated excitement often coupled with a heart stopping moment

Spiders weaving their webs around windows and doors, trying to catch their prey
People dressing up in scary costumes, witches, ghouls and movie favourites of the day
Children calling on friends and family, their hearts filled with delight
Knocking on the doors singing scary rhymes hoping to be rewarded with a treat

Decorating the house with cackling witches, spooky skeletons, laughing clowns and some coloured lights
Carving pumpkins and shaping into scary faces to be placed outside glowing bright
Roasting marshmallows, drinking hot chocolate and eating apple pie following family tradition
Playing games by the fireside and telling ghost stories and yarns of superstition

Watching fireworks, the roman candles and rockets as they rise so high
Mesmerised by the colours on display as they light up and brighten the sky
The awesome screeching, crackling and whooshing sounds shattering the silence of the night
Have a great Halloween but remain alert as you may just get an unexpected fright

Christmas Magic

Christmas is a wonderful festive time of the year
Catching up with family and friends, all those who we hold dear
Celebration of beautiful religious traditions established in bygone times
Modern day culture, heritage and beliefs closely entwined

The Christmas Star shines brightly in the dark winter sky
A guiding light helping all travellers keep safe on their journey
Church services with the Christmas Crib presented just as in Bethlehem
With the baby Jesus, Mary and Joseph, shepherds and the three wise men

A time for shopping and spending time admiring the beautiful items on display
Buying presents as a gesture of love and kindness for that special day
Santa visits the stores making sure he has all the latest games and toys
For his special delivery on Christmas Eve for the good little girls and boys

Putting up Christmas trees, real or artificial with bright glistening lights
Decorated with shiny baubles, delicate figurines and sweet delights
Elf on the shelf visiting the children and getting up to all sorts of mischief
Bringing such delight and happiness through their pranks and disarray

Crisp frosty mornings hopefully with a sprinkling of snow
To help Santa and his reindeer friends steer their sleigh with many miles to go
Visiting people letting them know how much they are cared about, not left alone
Enjoying the family celebrations and relaxing at home

The Christmas Angel

Each year as she sits on the top of the Christmas tree
It's the most wonderful place to be
With her radiant clothes and golden glow
Enjoying the view of all the Christmas festivity

A special time of the year filled with so much joy and cheer
Beautiful baubles and lights glistening and sparkling so clear
Families coming together to celebrate this wonderful time of the year
Seeing the happy couples kissing under the mistletoe

Children getting excited as they wait until Christmas Eve for Santa to appear
Laughter and celebrations and a beautiful food array
Watching the smiles and excitement on children's faces as they open their gifts
Singing of favourite carols, playing in the snow, so much not to be missed

Watching over the family as they prepare for this special day
Celebrating the story of the beautiful nativity
An opportunity to acknowledge and cherish those who we hold dear
Creating memories with those we haven't seen for a number of years

She has a limited time to support the Christmas theme
Her guidance is heaven sent to those who believe
Filling hearts with love and joy, so much happiness to achieve
Making life seem special and filled with hope and dreams

Gathering around the Christmas tree

The Christmas tree standing tall and upright in its rightful place
Located at the centre of the village square in a shared space
Filled with tinsel, baubles, coloured ribbons and candy sticks
Homemade decorations adding a touch of individuality, making it unique

Its branches reaching out offering all who view it a welcoming embrace
With its wonderful sparkling lights brightening up the area providing a sense of magic for all
With the bright golden star at the top guiding people home on a dark winter's eve
Excitement and glee as Santa arrives to place the children's presents under the tree

Beginning of the celebrations in preparation for the arrival of Christmas
Sharing good wishes with our neighbouring village families
Gathering of local people, friends and visitors to share in an evening of Christmas festivity
Standing around the tree creating a sense of belonging for all members of the community

Reflecting on our youthful memories from years gone by
Tinged with sadness as we remember those who are no longer here
Singing beautiful Christmas Carols merrily
Uniting people from all denominations, race and nationality

The Last Goodbye

As I walked down the long corridor
People passing by laughing and chatting
Going about their daily lives and activities
So caught up in their moment I'm not even seen
Barely able to place one foot in front of the other
Head bowed overcome with shock
Heart filled with utter disbelief
My troubles weighing heavily on my mind
How did it get to this point?
There were no warnings
No signs telling me changes were on the way
Their arrival has brought devastating impact
My mind and thoughts are jumbled
For the past few weeks I've been by your side
They said the operation was a success
You would make a full recovery
Alas it was not meant to be
I was just tidying your things when it happened
It fell to the floor
A little grey box, I'd never seen before
The lid was off so I reached down to replace it
I couldn't believe what was sitting in front of me
A photograph of you with another family
Standing with two beautiful children
The family resemblance painfully obvious to see
The shock had my head spinning
Feeling nauseous as to what the truth behind this could be
There hadn't been any clues previously
We'd been together for fifteen years
How naive I had seemingly been

I gathered up the box and put it back on the shelf safely
My loving wife I had just lost so tragically
What secret had you been hiding from me

My Irish Maiden

How I long once again my native Irish maiden to see
With her gorgeous emerald green lands so far away from me
I left so many years ago, my fortune to make when I was young and carefree
Her beautiful ballads and songs forever calling me to return to her safely

Her many rivers and loughs, waterfalls and seas, nature's real richness
Beautiful sandy beaches and hidden bays stretching for miles and miles
Glistening and dazzling under the rays of the rich golden sun
Her wonderful Irish treasure that she generously shares with everyone

A warm handshake with a céad míle fáilte to all who set foot on her cherished soil
Known for her beautiful forests, widely used for walks, so picturesque and serene
She holds out her arms protecting her coastlines from the harsh elements
They constantly batter against her but she remains strong and continues to uphold

Years of hard labour invested over generations, transforming and protecting her lands
Surviving great loss and hardship through the famine as her people suffered terribly
Shooting and bombs tearing down her structured walls and massacring her people
Bringing devastation and destruction to her lands as they fought for unwarranted control

The good people who work the land and those who fish her seas providing sustenance
The fishing vessels as they battle the choppy waters laden with heavy cargo upon return
The amazing teachers who work tirelessly for the education and fulfilment of our youth
Expanding my maiden's reach throughout the world where the Irish are inherently engrained

I long to hear sound of my maiden's beautiful Gaelic tongue once again
Lost in some areas due to persecution of its speakers by those who did not comprehend it
However, it has survived and destiny encourages her language to flourish
A land that has evolved over the years supporting many other languages and cultures

My health is poor and I'm too frail to travel any distance, sadly
My Irish maiden however, is held deep within my heart for eternity
A much different land from the one I left in the 1950s, now filled with modern technology
A land gifted with amazing people who hold their place across the world effectively

Imperfections

Born with a disability, visually impaired, or having a different gene
Sometimes clearly visible, however quite often remaining unseen
Skin imperfections such as rashes, birthmarks or uneven skin tone
Hidden away from the public eye, destined for a life alone

Young men in their prime off to war with their strong physique
Emancipated war-torn body no longer firm and muscular, now incomplete
Wounds inflicted from gun shells and bomb blasts shattering limbs
Life-changing with deep mental scarring making the future seem very grim

Car crash injuries causing the body to be damaged beyond repair
The devastating spinal impact resulting in the rest of life spent in a wheelchair
Restrictions of movement due to stroke, with facial distortion and broken speech
Enduring intense cancer treatment, hair loss, loss of identity, normal life hard to reach

Feeling of unworthiness, being unable to feed yourself or do own self-care
Loss of identity no longer being able to communicate the things you personally prefer
Undergoing humiliation as people continually mock and stare
Who defines perfection, denoting differences that really aren't there?

The Fitness Machine

Often delivered under the premise of no pain, no gain
It has become a well-established and refined machine
A highly competitive money making industry
Promoting certain body shapes to gain popularity

A product with widely marketed social media imagery
Sometimes preying on the vulnerable with low self-esteem
Trying desperately to get the perfect body, it would seem
Searching for happiness and content within their inner being

Making promises of quick fixes, body reduction
The new you and with happiness guaranteed
Perhaps taking a miracle pill each night before you sleep
Waking up the next day being pounds lighter and lean

Some are honest and dedicated to the regime
Helping people on their journey initiating self-belief
Supporting transformations and improved quality of life
Improving the individual's mental and physical wellbeing

Building their self-confidence while improving their health
Offering the opportunity to advance their hopes and dreams
Enabling them to reach their desired goals
Enhancing the person as a whole, making them feel complete

The Whisper

She heard it as a whisper
Softly spoken with gentle tones
Words gently floating along
Rustling like leaves in a light breeze
Urging her to come closer
Drawing her near
Slowly the mystery begins to unfold
Someone is calling her name
Guiding her towards a radiant light
Her heart is filled with fluttering
Her head is confused but there is no fear
She can feel the excitement build within
Beginning to realise what is happening
As everything becomes clear
The purpose of her journey now evident
Looking around she sees all those she held dear
It's been such a long time since they were so close
Her heart is no longer heavy and weak
The pain and grief has finally been released
She is being rewarded for her kindness
Her caring for others over the years
Her selfless actions and gestures of love
No longer filled with sadness or feeling alone
As she is awarded her seat at the heavenly throne

New Year Hopes

At the end of each year the mind jumps into action
Reflecting back to the same time in the previous year
Filled with thoughts of what ifs and what may have been
Resolutions that were made with such intent and determination

Now forgotten about, changing jobs, losing weight or getting active
Sometimes life has a habit of changing direction
So what, if it wasn't all achieved and you veered off track
Don't be so hard on yourself, you are not weak

Bringing unplanned joy to fruition realising an unexpected dream
Each year will bring its own challenges that will test our esteem
That doesn't mean you can't plan ahead, set targets deep within
The part that really matters is that we get to see a bright new year begin

School days

Should be the innocent time for youths eager to learn and grow
Positive little minds soaking up words, there's so much to know
Kind and loving teachers passing on their love for books
Building their knowledge of life, getting them positively hooked

Studying the worldwide globe, planning to visit far off lands
Guiding the children to make their future plans
Making happy memories enabling their individual personalities to shine
Building friendships with little boys and girls, their education entwined

Running around the playground playing games
Breaking rules, jumping dinner queues, no-one accepting the blame
Their youthful hearts filled with eagerness, a joy to see
Having friends for a sleepover and going to birthday parties

Sometimes school can be sad and distressing for children
Struggling to read and write, dreading each day
Being afraid or too anxious to speak or play
Dreadful ingrained memories, their innocent minds defiled

As some teachers are filled with impatience and disdain
Not allowing children with additional needs to grow at a pace of their own
Sometimes bitter and twisted actions inflicting darkness and pain
Growing up not fulfilling their potential such an unnecessary shame

Walk With Me

Walk with me my precious little one
Your new journey has just begun
Don't worry about the distance, it's not too far away
I'll be with you every step, from your side I will not stray

Lay your head gently on the pillow and hold teddy tight
Don't be afraid everything is going to be alright
Never complaining about your illness or the pain
I won't let you fall as I hold you close in my arms again

I'm proud of you my chosen one
Your suffering is nearly over, almost done
It's been amazing how you always kept your smile
I've been watching over you all this while

My angels have told me of your kindness and love
I've reserved a special place for you at my side up above
Helping to raise money for other children who are very unwell
Many will recover but only time will tell

You've carried your burden so silently
Your mum and dad will be sad, truly broken-hearted
But they will know that you are safe and happy, although departed
Flying with my heavenly angels for all eternity

Footprints in the snow

On a cold December night as the ground was covered with its first winter snow
People were rushing home hugging their coats tightly as the bitter wind began to blow
Street lights reflecting in the windows and smoky smells coming from warm fire embers now alight
Little birds finding shelter under the eaves getting settled down for the night

Someone was watching close by, waiting patiently for everyone to leave
Eyes darting around cautiously, trying to remain hidden with their identity concealed
Searching for leftover or unused food in upturned bins
Evidence of living on the streets, unkempt appearance and looking painfully thin

Aware of having limited time out in the open, hoping not to be discovered
Perils of the night, many types of predator best not uncovered
As daylight slowly arrives the footprints and tracks are all covered again with a fresh layer of snow
No one can be certain who did they belong to or in what direction did they go

Dancing with your Shadow

Mirror image of ourselves dancing by our side
Looking at our inner being with eyes open wide
Reflecting on our actions and moves
Distorting our silhouette, shaping our groove

Walking along playfully side by side in tranquil essence
Dramatically increasing or diminishing our presence
Sometimes stretching ahead or following directly behind
Fascinating patterns intertwined with body and mind

Existing as a shadow of yourself and lacking in self-esteem
Floating along not fulfilling your life or achieving your dreams
Just hanging in the balance, feeling delicate and only partially seen
Hiding in the background unable to reach out, find your voice or intervene

Others will try to discourage and hinder your success, things seem bleak
Trying to control your thoughts, making you vulnerable and weak
Ignore these negative and jealous influences trying to extinguish your light
Be strong and let the image of your shadow shine bright

Stand up for your beliefs and your shadow will gain in height
Cast off your demons, throw down the chains of life
Don't be afraid take a chance and reach up high
You will never be whole unless you try

Dance along with your shadow
Let your wonderful ideas and imagination flow
Realise your dreams, let them reach completion
Nothing is impossible, endless opportunities await, as you transition

The Lullaby

As you lie there sleeping silently my little one
Watching you my heart becomes undone
Listening to you breathing so gently
Sleep softly my sweet baby

Sweet dreams my precious child
Rest your tiny head for a little while
Stretch out your perfect little body
Sleep softly my sweet baby

A gift of absolute love
Beautifully formed and endeared
Innocent and free
Sleep softly my sweet baby

An amazing world awaits you
You can be whatever you wish to be
Life will be filled with so much opportunity
Sleep softly my sweet baby

Your light shines brightly like the stars
Sharing your angelic radiance
And gentle heart-warming smile
Sleep softly my sweet baby

A Time to Fly

Spread your wings
Raise them high
Soar way up into the sky
The world is out there waiting for you

Realise your dreams
Hold your breath and make your wishes come true
Open your eyes and mind to the endless possibilities for you
Let new beginnings start to unfold

Spread your wings
Raise them high
Soar way up into the sky
The world is out there waiting for you

Hold your head up high
Make your life rich with colour
Be yourself and light the flame within
Enjoy your life don't let time pass you by

Spread your wings
Raise them high
Soar way up into the sky
The world is out there waiting for you

Achieve your goals do not hesitate you will not fail
Trust in me let go of your pain
Don't shed any tears
Together we will overcome your fears

Spread your wings
Raise them high
Soar way up into the sky
The world is out there waiting for you

Don't mind the jeers and whispers
Let the rain wash away your worries
And the sun warm your heart
You are powerful and strong

Spread your wings
Raise them high
Soar way up into the sky
The world is out there waiting for you

You are beautiful and kind
Spread a little happiness wherever you tread
Smile and hold out your hands
The ground will hold you firm when you land

The Waterfall

The beauty of the Waterfall
Mother Nature sharing her glory with us all
A wonderful and magical vision
Weaving its way from mountaintop to riverbed with such precision

Plunging downwards as the water collides with rocks and hills
Fast flowing and rushing forward as it spills
Shaping and forming everything it touches as it flows along
Heavy rainfall making its current very strong

Found in places very tranquil and serene
A hidden gem that just has to be seen
Calming your heart and drawing you into its hold
A beautiful uplifting experience to behold

The Epitaph

What would the epitaph of my life say?
I accepted challenges, always willing to engage in new things
Wasn't afraid to step away from the crowds
Remained my own person despite facing ridicule
Respected others choices even when I didn't fully agree
Supported the vulnerable and those with the minority voices
Admitted being wrong in my understanding of situations
Held my ground steadfast overcoming external miscommunications
Protective of my family cherishing them for all eternity
A loyal and trustworthy friend upon which you could always depend
Loved a good hearty laugh and having fun
Quiet by nature but determined to succeed
Kept an open mind and was willing to implement change
Reputable in stature and firm in decision-making
A formidable leader as opposed to a meek follower
A good listener hearing what people actually had to say
Able to retain a secret not sharing it as gossip the following day
At least I tried my very best and put on quite a show

Farewell to another Year

As we reach the end of the year and wonder at the passing of time
Pausing a short while for reflection before Midnight's final chime
Many thoughts and memories springing to mind
Sadness and happiness indelibly intertwined

A year bearing so much, like a tree abundant with fruit heavily weighed down
Sometimes heart crushing and bringing our world crashing to the ground
The sun rises each morning sharing its warm golden rays
Showing us that each New Year offers its own beginnings and promise of better days

Rainbows majestically appear in the sky
Bright and radiant, beautiful and pleasing to our eye
Nature through its colourful seasonal displays providing symbols of hope
Lifting hearts and boosting energies, enabling us to adjust and cope

Acknowledgements

There are so many people who have supported me with the creation of my second book, the Gift of Time Poetry Collection. Firstly, a special word of thanks to my mum and extended family circle who continually inspire me and encourage me to create my poems and to share these with you the reader. My lifelong friends Margaret, Sheila and Theresa who are always at the end of the telephone line, giving me an honest opinion on the poems. I would like to thank my proof-reader Dessie who goes through the poetry in fine detail in advance of publication ensuring it is grammatically correct and suitable for public release. I would also like to thank the readers that have supported me through the purchase of my first book and their positive feedback has given me the confidence to continue writing. Finally, I would like to thank Orla Kelly Publishing for accepting my work and for their continuous support and professionalism in enabling me to get my new poetry collection, the Gift of Time to final publication.

About the Author

In October 2022 Susan had her first Poetry collection, The River of Life published. The welcome that this piece of work received encouraged Susan to work towards the release of another collection and she is delighted to be able to share this with you now. Having featured in local media including Ulster Herald, Local Women Magazine and in the Dergian online magazine. Susan is originally from Aghyaran near Castlederg, however, now lives in Drumquin, County Tyrone, Northern Ireland. Susan is a graduate of Ulster University having gained a BA (Hons) in Business Studies and also a Masters in Business Administration (MBA) and has worked in local government for over 25 years, working both with local businesses and the community and voluntary sector. Susan has a great love for the written word and poetry as it enables her to combine the beauty of language and nature with the emotional journey we experience throughout our lives.

Dear Reader,

Thank you for taking the time to read my poetry book. If you enjoyed it, I'd really appreciate if you'd tell others about it, and if you could leave a review in Goodreads or anywhere online – that would be great.

Thank you,

Susan

www.ingramcontent.com/pod-product-compliance
Lightning Source LLC
Chambersburg PA
CBHW042258280426
43661CB00097BA/1184